Looking at American Food

A pictorial introduction to American language and culture

Jann Huizenga

Photographs by
Kim Wm. Crowley
and
Jann Huizenga

VOLUNTAD PUBLISHERS, INC., a subsidiary of
NATIONAL TEXTBOOK COMPANY • **Lincolnwood, Illinois U.S.A.**

1985 Printing

Copyright © 1983 by Voluntad Publishers, Inc.,
a subsidiary of National Textbook Company
4255 West Touhy Avenue
Lincolnwood (Chicago), Illinois 60646-1975 U.S.A.
567890 ML 9876543

Contents

Introduction

Eating. It is one of the most important and interesting parts of our daily lives. In the following pages, you will take a look at eating customs in the United States and see what Americans eat, when they eat, how they eat, where they eat, and more. As you read about Americans and food, compare their customs with your own.

B.

A.

D.

POPCORN $.50
COTTON CANDY
STICK .75
BAG 1.00
SNO-KONES .50
CANDY APPLE .50
CARMEL APPLE

CANDY

C.

CAFE & COFFEE HOUSE FIGTREE'S CAFE

E.

F.

Sal's
Birdland Restaurant
B·B·Q CHICKEN
WINGS 7up
& RIBS

McDonald's
HAMBURGERS
DRIVE-THRU

McDonald's

The American Breakfast

On school and work days, breakfast in most American homes is often a hurried[1] meal of juice, coffee and toast or cereal. Some people skip[2] it completely in order to get to work or school on time. Others stop briefly at coffee shops for coffee and doughnuts,[3] America's favorite morning pastry.

On weekends, breakfasts are more leisurely[4] and often very large. When eaten late, a large breakfast is often called a "brunch," a combination of the words breakfast and lunch. Eggs, bacon, home-fried potatoes and toast are a popular breakfast combination. So are pancakes and sausage.

Many restaurants specialize in these two combinations and offer a "bottomless cup of coffee" as well.[5]

1. What foods are in pictures A and B?

2. Look at picture C. What is included with the breakfast special? What else can you have with it?

3. Which of the doughnuts in picture D would you choose?

1 hurried hasty, quick **2 skip** omit, not do **3 doughnut** a small, round cake fried in fat **4 leisurely** unhurried **5 as well** also

A.

B.

C.

D.

The American Lunch

A.

C.

In America, lunch is just a short break[1] from the day's activities rather than a serious, involved meal. It usually lasts only half an hour or an hour, so family members do not have time to return home. Americans frequently read or continue working during lunch break. The most standard lunch consists of a sandwich, a snack, and fruit or dessert. Working people either carry their lunches to work in the traditional[2] brown paper "lunch bag," or they eat a sandwich at a delicatessen (deli)[3] or lunch counter.[4] Cafeteria-style restaurants are also popular because of their quick self-service system. Most schools also have cafeterias, but many children prefer to bring the traditional "lunch box" filled by Mom.

1. Where are the people in pictures A and B?

2. What is the man carrying in picture C? What is probably inside it?

3. Where did the people in pictures D and E get their food?

1 break *interruption* **2 traditional** *usual, customary* **3 delicatessen (deli)** *a small grocery store which sells cooked meats and prepared salads* **4 lunch counter** *a place where light lunches are served*

E.

B.

D.

7

The American Dinner

Dinner is the principal meal of the day in the United States. This is the meal where the American family is most likely to sit down together. It is usually a hot, large meal as opposed to lunch, which is often cold and quick. Women have traditionally been in charge of preparing dinner. Nowadays, however, with more women working and as a result of "women's liberation," men are taking a more active role in the kitchen. Dinners throughout America differ greatly, but the standard meal consists of a meat dish, a vegetable, and potatoes, rice, or pasta.[1] Milk, water, and soft drinks[2] are common dinner beverages[3]; wine is served on special occasions. Dinner is usually eaten between 5 PM and 7 PM, and often later in restaurants.

1. What differences do you see between the dinners in pictures A and B?

2. Describe the meal in picture C.

3. Where are the husband and wife in picture D? What are they doing?

1 pasta *a paste or dough such as spaghetti, macaroni, etc.* **2 soft drink** *a carbonated, non-alcoholic drink* **3 beverage** *drink*

A.

PHOTO CREDIT: R. T. FRENCH COMPANY

B.

C.

D.

PHOTO CREDIT: R. T. FRENCH COMPANY

Fast Food

Because of the fast pace[1] of American life, many families do not have time to eat dinner together at the family table every evening. Many women have jobs. They don't always have time to make dinner, or they don't want to.

The most popular[2] type of restaurant serves fast foods such as hamburgers, hot dogs, pizza, fried chicken, tacos,[3] and french fries. Why are fast food restaurants so popular? First, they really are fast. You don't have to wait more than a minute or two for your food. They are also convenient.[4] You may dress casually,[5] and in some places you can even order[6] from your car and drive away with your food without going into the restaurant! Finally, fast food restaurants are inexpensive.[7] You can buy a complete meal in some fast food restaurants for less than two dollars.

A.

C.

1. What is happening in picture A?

2. Where are the people in picture B?

3. What is the man in picture C doing?

4. What kind of food does the stand in picture D probably serve?

1 pace *speed* **2 popular** *favorite* **3 tacos** *a Mexican food* **4 convenient** *easy to use* **5 casually** *informally, not dressed up* **6 order** *ask for* **7 inexpensive** *cheap*

B.

D.

Convenience Foods

Instead of buying only fresh foods, Americans nowadays buy many more convenience foods. These are foods which are already partly or completely prepared. Many of them are frozen,[1] such as frozen dinners ("TV dinners"), heat-and-serve French fries, and frozen pizzas. There are also many canned[2] convenience foods, such as ready-made spaghetti, soups, stews, and vegetables.

Convenience foods save time and trouble. They are popular with people who are busy or who don't like to cook or wash dishes. But they often cost more than fresh, un-prepared foods and may contain artificial additives.[3] Also, many people feel they don't taste as good as home-cooked foods.

1. What is included in each dinner in picture A?

2. What kinds of frozen foods do you see in picture B?

3. Look at picture C. What kind of dinner is the person going to eat?

1 frozen *made very cold* **2 canned** *put in a can* **3 artificial additive** *a chemical added to the food*

A.

C.

B.

Health Foods and Co-ops

In the 1960s, a "back-to-the-earth" movement was started by young people in the United States. The movement was a reaction against the harmful effects of technology. From the movement came a new understanding of food and health. Many people now prefer natural and organic[1] foods to the prepared foods sold in supermarkets. They buy natural foods in health food stores and in food co-ops, which are small community stores where customers[2] help manage the store. In co-ops, food is usually not packaged. Customers bring their own bags and jars and scoop their food out of bins[3] or baskets.[4]

1. What kinds of food do you see in picture A? Which ingredients do these products not have?

2. What kinds of products are sold in the store in picture B? What is on special sale this week?

3. What is the customer in picture C doing?

1 organic *chemical-free* **2 customer** *shopper, buyer* **3 bin** *a large, enclosed storage space* **4 basket** *a lightweight, woven container made of wood*

A.

B.

C.

15

The Diet Craze[1]

These days Americans are more and more concerned with watching their weight. Perhaps as many as 70 million Americans are on weight-reducing diets, and weight control has become a multibillion-dollar business. American supermarkets sell a variety of diet foods such as diet soft drinks, diet candy, and diet salad dressings. Dieters also spend money on diet pills, exercise machines, and jogging suits. Each year dozens of new diets are popularized. They have such names as the Miracle[2] Diet, the Nine-Day Wonder Diet, and the Easy 24-Hour Diet. There is even one called the Ice Cream Diet, which advises the dieter to eat only ice cream for lunch and dinner! For dieters who cannot lose weight on their own, there are many well-organized diet groups, which offer help and encouragement.

1. What do the diet drinks in picture A *not* contain?

2. What kinds of diet foods are shown in picture B?

3. Look at the diet books in picture C. Try to understand each title.

1 craze *mania, fashion* **2 miracle** *a supernatural event*

B.

A.

C.

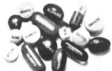
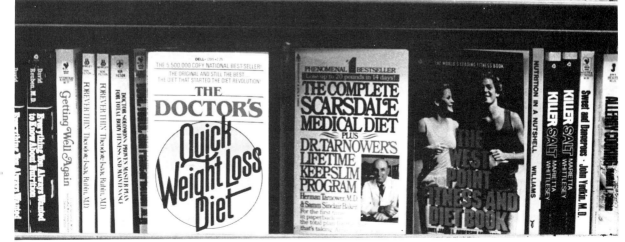

Ethnic[1] Eating

America is composed of many different nationality groups. These ethnic groups are proud of their cultural traditions and keep them alive in their cooking. As a result, American food is a mixture of cooking from all parts of the globe. Ethnic pride is displayed in the many popular ethnic food festivals held in towns and cities throughout the United States. At these festivals, foods from all over the world can be sampled[2]: Swedish meatballs, Greek salads, Russian borscht, German sausages, and much more. The diversity of food in America is most evident in its cities. There you can find ethnic restaurants of all varieties. Among the most common are Chinese, Italian, French, and Mexican restaurants.

1. Name five nationality groups represented in the pictures.

2. What are the specialties offered at the booth in picture A? Describe them.

3. Where are the people in picture D? How are they eating their food?

1 ethnic *relating to nationalities or races* **2 sampled** *tried, tasted*

C.

B.

PHOTO CREDIT: RAYMOND F. HILLSTROM

PHOTO CREDIT: RAYMOND F. HILLSTROM

A.

D.

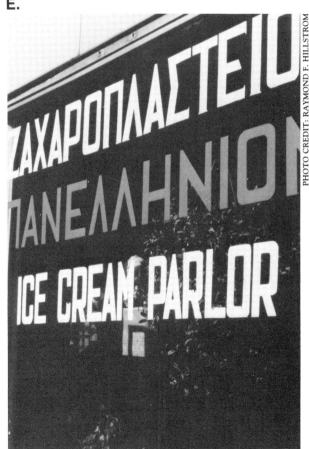

E.

Celebrating with Cake

In the United States, celebrations and ceremonies call for cake. Birthdays, weddings, wedding anniversaries, showers,[1] and receptions are not complete without a special cake. Cakes are often beautifully decorated with candy flowers, frosting[2] faces, or plastic toys. Written messages such as HAPPY ANNIVERSARY DARLING also commonly appear on cakes. Smiling bride[3] and groom[4] dolls or a pair of love birds decorate the tops of traditional tall white wedding cakes. Candles[5] are always placed on birthday cakes, and the birthday person must make a secret wish[6] before blowing them all out together.

1. What is the person in picture A celebrating?

2. Who are the people in picture B? What are they celebrating? Describe their cake.

3. What kind of cakes are in picture C? Who are they probably for?

1 shower *a party given for someone by friends who give gifts; baby showers and wedding showers are very common* **2 frosting** *a paste made of sugar and butter and put on the top of cakes* **3 bride** *a woman about to be married or just married* **4 groom** *a man about to be married or just married* **5 candle** *a piece of wax and string which is burned to give light* **6 make a wish** *hope or pray for something one wants*

A.

B.

C.

Screaming for Ice Cream

"I scream,[1] you scream, we all scream for ice cream." This popular old chant expresses the passion that Americans have for ice cream, the national dessert. Americans eat much more ice cream per person than any other nation. They eat it year round, even in the coldest winter weather. Every imaginable flavor[2] and fruit is put into ice cream.

Ice cream comes in many different forms. On top of a cone, it is called an "ice cream cone." Mixed with soda water and a flavoring, it is an "ice cream soda." Mixed with milk, it is a "shake." And topped with chocolate, strawberries, whipped cream or nuts, it is a "sundae." But the king of ice cream desserts is the "banana split." It is made with banana, scoops[3] of ice cream, chocolate syrup, whipped cream, nuts and cherries.

1. What are the people in pictures A, B and C eating?

2. Look at the menu in picture D. How much does a regular banana split cost? Is it the largest ice cream dish available? How much does a chocolate ice cream soda cost?

1 scream *shout or call loudly and intensely* **2 flavor** *a substance that gives food a particular taste and smell* **3 scoop** *a large spoonful*

A.

B.

C.

D.

Fountain Creations

GIANT BOSTON SODAS

Topped with Pure Whipped Cream
and a Maraschino Cherry. Sugar
Wafers.

STRAWBERRY 1.95

PINEAPPLE 1.95

CHOCOLATE 1.95

CHERRY 1.95

ROOT BEER 1.95

VANILLA 1.95

GIANT SUNDAE DELIGHTS

Topped with Pure Whipped Cream,
Nuts, Maraschino Cherry. Wafers.

HOT FUDGE 1.75

STRAWBERRY 1.75

CRUSHED PINEAPPLE 1.75

CHOCOLATE 1.75

BANANA SPLIT 3.25

Three Scoops of Assorted Ice Cream
Flavors and Topping, Sliced Banana,
Pure Whipped Cream, Chopped
Nuts, Maraschino Cherry and
Sugar Wafers.

BANANA ROYAL 2.50

Two Scoops of Ice Cream and
Assorted Syrups (no Fudge Sauce),
Sliced Banana, Whipped Cream,
Chopped Nuts, a Maraschino
Cherry and Sugar Wafers.

OLD FASHIONED SHAKES/MALTS

Served with Cookies.

TRIPLE RICH MILK SHAKE 1.75

TRIPLE RICH MALTED MILK . . . 1.95

Summertime Fun Foods

In June, July, and August, special foods which mark the festive summertime spirit appear all over America. On city streets or beaches,[1] at festivals and in parks, people nibble on[2] these foods as they walk or play. The foods are prepared so that they can be carried and eaten without much mess.[3] Ice cream is put into cones, candy apples are stuck onto sticks, and sugar is spun around a paper cone to make "cotton candy." Crushed[4] ice is flavored and put into paper cones to create "snow cones." Popcorn and peanuts are carried in bags or boxes. Corn is boiled,[5] buttered, salted, and eaten directly from the cob. Watermelon[6] is simply cut into pieces and eaten by hand down to the rind.[7]

1. What is the boy in picture A buying?

2. What are the women in picture B eating?

3. What is the couple in picture C eating?

4. What is being sold in picture D?

1 beach *the shore of an ocean, sea, or lake covered by sand or small stones* **2 nibble on** *to eat in small bits* **3 mess** *a dirty or untidy condition* **4 crushed** *broken into small pieces* **5 boiled** *cooked in hot water* **6 watermelon** *a very large fruit which is hard and green on the outside and red and watery on the inside, with many black seeds* **7 rind** *the hard outer layer*

A.

B.

C.

D.

Cowboy Cooking

Cooking outdoors on a charcoal grill is a favorite tradition all over the United States. From coast[1] to coast, you can see charcoal grills in almost every family's backyard in the summertime. Large cookouts are the center of activities. Family reunions, company picnics, church picnics and community festivals are not complete without grilled steaks, hamburgers, hot dogs, or chicken. Outdoor cooking began in the old American Wild West, where the cowboys cooked their meals over open fires. Today the father in the city or the suburbs plays the part of the cowboy.

1. Describe the scene in picture A. What are the men doing?

2. Where are the people in pictures B, C, and D? What are they cooking?

1 **coast** *the land next to an ocean or a sea*

B.

A.

C.

D.

Thanksgiving Day

Thanksgiving Day is the American holiday most often associated with food. On this day, the fourth Thursday in November, Americans prepare a feast[1] and give thanks for all they have. Thanksgiving Day is an old tradition. It was first celebrated in Massachusetts in 1621 by the Pilgrims.[2] They gathered together with Indians to thank God for a rich harvest.[3]

Thanksgiving is a time for family reunions. Parents, children, and grandchildren often travel long distances to be together for the special meal. The traditional roast turkey,[4] which is carved[5] at the table, is the main attraction of the meal. Other traditional foods include cranberry[6] sauce, sweet potatoes, and, for dessert, pumpkin[7] pie.

1. What foods can you see on the Thanksgiving table in picture A?

2. What are the large birds in picture B, and what will probably happen to them?

3. What is the man in picture C doing?

1 feast *a very large meal* **2 Pilgrims** *the English settlers who landed at Plymouth, Massachusetts in 1620* **3 harvest** *a crop of fruit and grain* **4 turkey** *a type of large bird* **5 carved** *cut with a knife* **6 cranberry** *a bright red, acid berry* **7 pumpkin** *a large, orange-colored fruit of a vine*

A.

B.

C.

Table Manners, American Style

There are several ways in which American dining customs differ from those elsewhere. An invited dinner guest is expected to arrive at the specified time, contrary to the customs in some countries. The use of the knife and fork is often different. The fork is used mostly in the right hand. It gathers the food without help from the knife, which is generally used only to cut meat and potatoes, and is to the right of the plate when not in use. And while in many places the napkin[1] is put around the neck, here it is put on the lap.[2] Finally, Americans tend to eat some foods with their fingers. At informal dinners and picnics, chicken, corn-on-the-cob, pizza and tortillas[3] are eaten without utensils.[4]

1. Where is the napkin in picture A?

2. Describe the utensils in picture B.

3. What kind of meal are the people in picture C having, and how are they eating it?

4. How is the man eating corn-on-the-cob in picture D?

1 napkin *cloth or paper used to clean the lips and hands at the table* **2 lap** *the top part of the legs of a seated person* **3 tortillas** *a Mexican food* **4 utensils** *knives, forks, and spoons*

A.

B.

C.

D.

31

Restaurant Rules

American restaurant customs are somewhat different from those in other countries. Elsewhere, it may be appropriate to get a waiter or waitress' attention by calling, whistling,[1] or snapping the fingers. In America, you put up a finger to catch his or her eye.

In many parts of the world a fixed service charge is added to restaurant bills.[2] In most American restaurants it is common to tip[3] the waiter or waitress about 15% of the total bill. If the service was very good, you can leave a larger tip. If it was bad, you may leave less. The tip is usually left on the table, but you can also give it directly to the waiter or waitress.

In better restaurants you pay your bill through the waitress or waiter. In inexpensive ones, you pay at the cash register.

Finally, if you are not able to finish your food, it is perfectly acceptable to ask for a "doggie bag" for the extra food.

1. In picture A, how is the customer getting the waitress' attention?

2. Look at the tip in picture B. What was the approximate total of the bill?

3. What sort of restaurant is the one in picture C?

1 whistling *making a sound by blowing air through the lips* **2 restaurant bill** *a statement of charges for food and drink* **3 tip (v)** *give a small amount of money for a service*

B.

A.

C.

33

Supermarket Sense

If you plan to shop in an American supermarket, follow these suggestions. Before you go shopping, look in the newspaper for coupons[1] for the items you want to buy. You can save money by giving them to the cashier before you pay. To find a specific item, check the large signs above each aisle.[2] They list what is available and will help you find what you need more quickly. You should be aware of brand names.[3] Most supermarkets carry a store brand, a generic brand,[4] and several others. Those two brands are usually the cheapest, although their quality may vary. Finally, if you are buying only a few items, you may enter the checkout lane[5] marked "express." This will save you from waiting behind customers with full carts.[6]

1. Who are the people in picture A and what are they doing?

2. Describe what you see in picture B.

3. Name three specific things you can buy in aisle 7 in picture C.

4. What is picture D, and what can you do with it?

5. What brand are the cereals in picture E?

1 coupon *a ticket which is worth money* **2 aisle** *a passageway* **3 brand name** *the name of the manufacturer* **4 generic brand** *a general brand which is not connected with any particular manufacturer* **5 checkout lane** *the place in a supermarket where you pay for your goods* **6 cart** *a small vehicle with wheels*

A.

B.

C.

D.

E.

Other Food Sources

Large, impersonal supermarkets are not the only place in the United States to buy groceries.[1] There are small co-ops, health food stores, and delis. There are also drive-in markets and 24-hour mini-markets, which are convenient but more expensive than supermarkets. In addition, most towns and cities have daily[2] or weekly outdoor farmers' markets, where you can buy fresh fruit and vegetables directly from the farmer. In the summertime, small, private vegetable stands[3] appear all along roadways in rural America.

The neighborhood butcher shop,[4] fruit and vegetable shop, and bakery[5] are not as common as in the past, but they still exist in ethnic urban areas.

Look at each of the four pictures. What kind of market do you see in each?

1 groceries *food supplies* **2 daily** *every day* **3 stand** *an open-air structure* **4 butcher shop** *a shop which sells meat* **5 bakery** *a shop which sells bread and other baked goods*

A.

B.

C.

D.

Food Production in America: Fruits and Vegetables

California's fertile,[1] irrigated[2] valleys produce far more fruits and vegetables than those of any other state. Its climate is mild, so tomatoes, lettuce, artichokes, and oranges grow there year round. Much of this is exported to other states and countries. California also has many vineyards, which produce about 80% of America's wine. Florida, with California, grows most of the nation's citrus fruits.[3] Washington, in the Northwest, is well known for its Red Delicious apples. Idaho, just to the east, is famous for its big, tasty potatoes. And Hawaii, 3,200 kilometers out in the Pacific, produces the most tropical fruits, such as pineapples, bananas, and coconuts.

1. Describe the land in picture A.

2. What produce do you see in pictures B and C? What states did it come from?

3. Look at picture D. What is happening to this American produce? Where did it probably come from?

1 fertile *productive, rich* **2 irrigated** *watered artificially*
3 citrus fruits *oranges, grapefruit, lemons, and limes*

PHOTO CREDIT: CALIFORNIA CANNERS AND GROWERS

A.

B.

C.

D.

Food Production in America: Grains

The two major grain-producing areas in the United States are called the Corn Belt and the Wheat Belt. The Corn Belt is centered in the Midwestern states of Iowa and Illinois and extends into seven other states. Its black soil[1] and long hot summers are also good for growing soybeans, alfalfa, and oats. Field corn is used for animal feed, cereal and oil. Wheat is grown mainly in the Great Plains and in Oregon and Washington. Kansas, in the center of the Great Plains, is the leading wheat-producing state. Flat fields and red barns[2] beneath tall silos[3] fill the landscape of both Belts. Agriculture there is highly mechanized; large machines do everything from preparing the soil to harvesting the crop.

1. What is happening in picture A?

2. Describe the scenes in pictures B and C.

1 soil *earth* **2 barn** *a large building used to house farm animals and equipment* **3 silo** *a cylinder used to store animal feed* **4 harvest a crop** *gather together mature grain or fruit*

A.

PHOTO CREDIT: CALIFORNIA CANNERS AND GROWERS

B.

C.

Food Production in America: Meat, Fish, and Dairy

Americans eat a lot of meat; on the average, they consume well over 150 pounds (68 kilograms) a year. By far the most popular meat in America is beef.[1] Most beef cattle are raised on large ranches in Texas, Oklahoma, and other western states and are then shipped to the Midwest for final fattening on grain. The second most common meat in America is pork.[2] Hogs are raised mostly in the Midwestern Corn Belt states because corn is the primary hog food.

Seafood is most popular in areas along the Atlantic and Pacific Coasts and near the Gulf of Mexico. Maine lobster, West Coast salmon, crab, and oysters, and Florida shrimp are just some of the well-known regional delicacies.[3]

Dairy products—milk, cheese, cottage cheese, butter, cream, etc.—come primarily from cattle raised in the Dairy Belt, an area which stretches from New England to New York State and on to Wisconsin, Iowa, and Minnesota. Wisconsin, especially famous for its numerous cheeses, has long been the leading dairy state.

1. Where are the cattle in picture A? What are they doing?

2. What is the general name for the foods in picture B? Try to give specific names for as many items as you can.

3. What is the man in picture C selling? Where did they probably come from?

1 **beef** *meat from a cow* 2 **pork** *meat from a hog*
3 **delicacy** *a food that is pleasing and considered luxurious*

A.

B.

PHOTO CREDIT: UNITED DAIRY INDUSTRY ASSOCIATION

Menus

1. Look at Menu A.
   - (a) How many meat dishes does this restaurant serve? How many seafood dishes?
   - (b) You order a baked onion soup, spinach salad, pork chops with apple sauce and potato pancake, and no dessert. What will your total bill be?
   - (c) Approximately how much should you tip your waiter or waitress?

2. Look at Menu B.
   - (a) At which meal are these foods generally eaten?
   - (b) How many different kinds of hamburgers are offered?
   - (c) When you order any of these sandwiches, what else will be served on the plate with it?

3. Look at Menu C.
   - (a) At which meal are these foods generally eaten?
   - (b) Name the meats on the menu. Are they served alone?

DINNER MENU

Choice of (1) Soup Du Jour — Onion Soup — Baked Onion Soup 1.00 extra

Choice of (1) Tossed Salad — Cole Slaw — Blue Cheese .75 extra

Our Special Spinach Salad with Hot Bacon Dressing .75 extra

Choice of Potato — French Fries — Baked — Potato Pancake or Vegetable

HOUSE SPECIALTIES

Breaded Pork Tenderloin — served with apple sauce . 5.95

Wienerschnitzel à la Holstein 7.95
served with our special tomato sauce and a fried egg

Prime Rib Eye of Beef 9.95
dry aged and slowly roasted

1/2 Spring Fed Chicken 5.95
any way you want it — broiled or pan fried

Calves Liver 6.95
either sauteed or broiled —served with grilled onions and bacon

Chicken Kiev 6.95
fresh chicken breast, stuffed with butter and parsley — served with rice pilaf

Beef en Brochette 7.95
beef tenderloin with tomato, green pepper, onion and mushroom — served with rice pilaf

BBQ Baby Back Ribs with our special sauce 8.95

Chateaubriand for Two 22.95
garnished with duchess potato, tomato Parisienne and broccoli

Old Fashioned Breaded Pork Chops —apple sauce . 7.95

French Fried Shrimp —tangy cocktail sauce 6.95

Australian Lobster Tail 16.95

Alaskan King Crab —split for easy eating 11.95

Turf and Surf 16.95

A. Crab Legs and Steak 13.95

Super Sandwiches

All Gold Coin Super Sandwiches are Served with Idaho French Fried Potatoes, Cole Slaw and a Pickle on a Toasted Bun.

SUPER HAMBURGER 2.75
Ground Beef.

SUPER CHEESEBURGER 2.95
With American Cheese.

SUPER OLIVEBURGER 3.10
With Chopped Stuffed Olives.

SUPER BEEF with BBQ Sauce 3.45
A Generous Portion of Beef, covered with our Special Bar-B-Q Sauce, on a Toasted Bun, Idaho French Fried Potatoes, Cole Slaw and a Pickle.

REUBEN SANDWICH 3.75
On Pumpernickel Bread, Corned Beef, Swiss Cheese, Sauerkraut, 1000 Island Dressing, French Fries, Cole Slaw, and a Pickle. Served Open Faced.

SUPER CORNED BEEF 4.50
Served with French Fried Potatoes, Cole Slaw and a Pickle.

SUPER ROAST BEEF 4.50
Very Good.

SUPER RIBEYE STEAK 5.95

FAMOUS SUPER FRANCHEEZIE . . 3.25
A Pure Beef Frankfurter stuffed with Melted Cheese, Wrapped in Bacon, on a Toasted Roll, Cole Slaw, French Fried Potatoes.

SUPER PIZZABURGER 3.25
Mellow Mozzarella Cheese over Ground Beef, with Italian Sauce. Served with French Fries, Cole Slaw, Pickle. On an English Muffin.

Other Sandwiches

JUMBO BEEF SUBMARINE 4.25
On a King Size Vienna Roll, served with Creamy Cole Slaw and a Pickle.

BROILED RIBEYE STEAK 5.95
Served on Pumpernickel Bread, with Cole Slaw and a Pickle.

SARDINE SANDWICH 2.25
Served on Pumpernickel Bread, with Creamy Cole Slaw and a Pickle.

C.

All Time Favorites

Fried Potatoes, Toast, Butter and Jelly served with all Egg orders.

PURE CORNED BEEF HASH AND 2 EGGS 3.75
Any Style Eggs.

SCRAMBLED EGGS AND ONIONS 2.75

TWO COUNTRY FRESH EGGS . . . 2.10

With Bacon 2.75

With Sausage 2.75

With Ham 2.95

With Canadian Bacon 2.95

OMELETTES

Cheese 2.75

Ham 3.25

Ham and Cheese 3.50

Denver 3.75

Spanish 3.50

Pancakes and Waffles

Served with Butter and Syrup We serve Dietetic Syrup if desired.

THREE GOLDEN BROWN WHEATCAKES 2.75

POTATO PANCAKES 3.50
Served with Sour Cream or Applesauce.

WAFFLE 1.75

FRENCH TOAST 2.75

HAM STEAK AND EGGS (2)

TWO COUNTRY FRESH EGGS . . . 4.50

RIBEYE STEAK AND EGGS (2) . . . 6.25

Above Eggs Served "Any Style."

COLD CEREALS

With Milk 1.25

With Half and Half 1.25

NTC ESL/EFL TEXTS AND MATERIAL

Stepping into English Series
(filmstrip/audiocassette/book/
  duplicating masters)
    The City Mouse and the Country
      Mouse
    The Lion and the Mouse
    The Rabbit and the Turtle
    The Boy Who Cried Wolf
    Belling the Cat
    The Milkmaid and Her Pail
    Goldilocks and the Three Bears
    The Little Red Hen
    The Boy and the Donkey

*The English Survival Series
Building Vocabulary A, B, C
Identifying Main Ideas A, B, C
Recognizing Details A, B, C
Writing Sentences and Paragraphs
  A, B, C

*Everyday English 1, 2, 3, 4

Duplicating Masters
Easy Vocabulary Games
Play and Practice!
Basic Vocabulary Builder
Practical Vocabulary Builder

Language Skills Material
*Easy English Learning Cards
*Easy English Activities Book
Language Visuals (flash cards)

Computer Software
Basic Vocabulary Builder on Computer

Read-A-Long with the Story Teller
(24 cassette/book packages of the best-
  loved fairy tales)
    Cinderella
    Hansel and Gretel
    Tom Thumb
    Jack & the Beanstalk
    Aladdin
    Rumpelstilskin
    Sleeping Beauty
    Snow White
    Little Red Riding Hood
    Pinocchio
    Ugly Duckling
    Elves & the Shoemaker
    Three Little Pigs/Goldilocks &
      the Three Bears
    Rapunzel/The Gingerbread Man
    Thumbelina
    Beauty & the Beast
    Bremen Town Musicians
    The Selfish Giant
    The Little Mermaid
    Steadfast Tin Soldier
    Puss in Boots
    The Wizard of Oz
    Gulliver's Travels
    Sinbad the Sailor

*Published by Voluntad Publishers, Inc.,
a subsidiary of National Textbook
Company

For further information or a current catalog, write:
National Textbook Company
4255 West Touhy Avenue
Lincolnwood, Illinois 60646-1975 U.S.A.